The Ultimate
Taylor Swift
Fan Book

100+ Facts, Quiz,
Photos + More

Jamie Anderson

BELLANOVA

MELBOURNE · SOFIA · BERLIN

Copyright © 2022 by Jamie Anderson

The Ultimate Taylor Swift Fan Book 2022
www.bellanovabooks.com

All rights reserved. No part of this book may be reproduced in any form by any electronic or mechanical means including photocopying, recording, or information storage and retrieval without permission in writing from the author.

Taylor Swift was not involved in the writing of this book. However, all facts are believed to be truthful based on reputable, public domain sources.

Photos licensed by Shutterstock.com

ISBN: 978-1-4710-1180-1
Imprint: Lulu.com

Contents

Introduction	4
Taylor: Fun Facts	6
Taylor: The Quiz	50
Early Life	50
Music	60
Private Life	72
Everything Else	80
Taylor: The Lyrics Quiz	88
Answers	96
Taylor: Quotes	98
Word search	110
Crossword Puzzle	112
Solutions	114
Coloring Pages	116

Taylor Swift
INTRODUCTION

Taylor Swift hit the music scene over 15 years ago, and she is still one of the world's biggest and most talented stars!

After releasing two of the bestselling albums of 2020, Taylor didn't disappoint in 2021. She fought back in true Taylor style and re-released many of her best hits, among many of other things. In this 2022 edition of *Taylor Swift: The Ultimate Unofficial Fan Book,* you have the chance to test your knowledge of Taylor and learn some new things about her.

Are you ready? Let's go!

Taylor Swift
FUN FACTS

Taylor used MySpace to launch her country music career.

• • •

Taylor has won 11 Grammy Awards, including *Album of the Year* in 2021. She was the youngest person ever to win *Album of the Year*.

• • •

In 2021, Taylor had over 9.1 BILLION streams on Spotify—the most of any female artist.

THE ULTIMATE TAYLOR SWIFT FAN BOOK

"I'm thankful that when I go to bed at night, that I have been myself that day. And I have been myself all the days before that."

— *Taylor Swift*

Taylor was obsessed with the show *Grey's Anatomy* and cried when Denny died.

• • •

When Taylor was 13, she wrote a 350-page novel, which has never been published.

• • •

Taylor put a photo of Kanye West interrupting her at the VMA's above her fireplace in Nashville with the caption *"life is full of little interruptions."*

• • •

Taylor has a driving license, but she has said that driving scares her as she's been in three accidents.

As of 2022, Taylor Swift was worth $570 million.

• • •

In 2022, Taylor became the first artist in history to have eight albums chart for at least 100 weeks on the Billboard 200.

• • •

Taylor owns a private jet worth $40 million, which she keeps at Nashville Airport.

• • •

Taylor's style inspiration comes from movie stars such as Audrey Hepburn and Brigitte Bardot.

Taylor recently said her favorite lyric she's ever written was *'Darling I'm a nightmare dressed like a daydream.'*

• • •

Taylor has really bad eyesight and needs to wear glasses or contact lenses.

• • •

In 2022, Taylor released, *Carolina*, an original song for the movie *Where the Crawdads Sing* and it broke the record for the biggest debut by an original soundtrack song on Spotify.

• • •

Taylor has won more Grammy Awards than any other woman.

Taylor uses chocolate milkshake as a dipping sauce for French fries.

• • •

Her song *Begin Again* was the first to knock *Gangnam Style* off the top of the charts.

• • •

Continuing with her love for the number 13, fans believe the release date of *Lover* was on 8/23 because 8+2+3 = 13.

• • •

Taylor prefers to play electric guitars to acoustic ones.

Taylor wrote all the songs on her *Speak Now* album herself.

• • •

When Taylor was 19 she had a framed photo of country singer George Strait in her bathroom.

• • •

Taylor memorized all the lyrics to Ellie Goulding's album *Halcyon*.

• • •

Taylor was the youngest person to feature in the *Forbes Celebrity 100* listing in 2015, and also ranked number one in 2019.

In 2009, Taylor had a part in an episode of *CSI: Crime Scene Investigation*.

• • •

Taylor always reserves the fifth spot on each album for her most emotional song.

• • •

Ronnie Kremer was Taylor's first guitar teacher, and inspired her to write her first song *Lucky You* when she was 12.

• • •

In 2018, Taylor featured on Sugarland's *Babe*, from their *Bigger* album.

> "In life, you learn *lessons*. And sometimes you learn them the *hard* way. Sometimes you learn them too late."
>
> — *Taylor Swift*

In 2019, Taylor signed to a new record label—*Republic Records and Universal Music Group*—after being with her last label for 13 years.

• • •

Taylor has three cats: Doctor Meredith Gray, Sargent Olivia Benson and Benjamin Button.

• • •

Taylor's cat Benjamin Button featured in her video for *Me!*. She said: "*He's the best little guy.*"

Taylor's penthouse in New York was previously owned by *Lord of the Rings* director, Peter Jackson.

• • •

Taylor uses social media and music videos to send 'Easter Eggs' that are cryptic clues about her upcoming music. How many have you spotted?!

• • •

Taylor wore a jacket covered in pins on the cover of *Entertainment Weekly*, and she said each pin was a clue about her new album *Lover*.

THE ULTIMATE TAYLOR SWIFT FAN BOOK

"It's hard to *fight* when the fight ain't *fair*."

— Taylor Swift

While recording her album *Reputation*, Taylor unfollowed everyone on Instagram and Twitter.

• • •

Folklore was the best-selling album in the USA in 2020.

• • •

Taylor is the first artist to have the best-selling album in five different years: *Fearless* in 2008, *1989* in 2014, *Reputation* in 2017, *Lover* in 2019, and *Folklore* in 2020.

Taylor auditioned for the role of Eponine in the film *Les Miserables* but lost out to Amanda Seyfriend.

• • •

Taylor never spoke about politics until 2018, when she asked her Instagram followers not to vote for a candidate who was against gay marriage.

• • •

Taylor rode horses competitively until she was 12 years old.

As well as playing a role in the movie *Cats*, Taylor cowrote the film's main song.

•••

Folklore was the first album Taylor recorded at home. She called the studio she built '*Kitty Committee Studios*' after her cats.

•••

Taylor didn't tell her record label she had recorded *Folklore* until a week before she released it!

On her *Folklore* album, a mystery co-writer called William Bowery turned out to be her boyfriend, Joe Alwyn.

• • •

When *Evermore* reached number one, Taylor broke the Guinness World Record for the shortest time between number one albums.

• • •

The first song Taylor learned to play on guitar was 'Kiss Me'.

Taylor's 2022 single *Carolina* was recorded in one take using only instruments that were available before 1953.

• • •

Taylor's 2012 hit *All Too Well* was originally ten minutes long. It was cut down to five minutes for her *Red* album. However, in 2021, Taylor released the full 10-minute version, along with an accompanying short film!

• • •

In 2021 *All Too Well* became the longest song in history to reach number one on the Billboard Hot 100.

In 2021, Taylor became the first female artist to win the *Artist of the Year* Grammy Award three times.

• • •

In 2021, Taylor broke the record for the longest song performed live on *Saturday Night Live.*

• • •

Although Taylor writes all her own music, she often works with collaborators. Her main collaborator is Jack Antonoff.

Taylor has double-jointed elbows!

• • •

Taylor turned off comments on her social media accounts because *"social media can be great, but it can also inundate your brain with images of what you aren't, how you're failing, or who is in a cooler locale than you at any given moment."*

• • •

In 2019, Taylor surpassed Michael Jackson's record of winning the most *American Music Awards*. So far, she has 34!

When she was younger, Taylor wanted to be a stockbroker like her dad.

• • •

Taylor is a huge fan of the comedienne Phoebe Waller-Bridge. She told *Entertainment Weekly*, "She makes you crack up, shocks you, and breaks your heart all in the span of a few minutes in that show." She then got to perform beside her on SNL!

• • •

When Taylor appeared on *Saturday Night Live*, she wrote her own monologue—which most celebrities aren't allowed to do.

Taylor is a godmother to Jaime King's son Leo Thames.

• • •

Taylor said in an interview that her favourite lyrics from her *Lover* album are: "Ladies and gentlemen, will you please stand? / With every guitar string scar on my hand/I take this magnetic force of a man to be my lover."

• • •

Taylor drinks her white wine with ice cubes.

Grow up one year at a time. Get **excited** about the things you're excited about, and *live life* one year at a time."

— *Taylor Swift*

In the music video for *Willow*, which was filmed during the COVID-19 pandemic, all the dancers' faces were hidden because they were wearing masks.

• • •

When Taylor released her song *Love Story (Taylor's Version)*, she joined Dolly Parton to be the only artist ever to have a number one hit with two versions of the same song.

• • •

Taylor wrote the song *Happiness* just one week before her album *Folklore* was released.

Taylor said she's obsessed with true crime podcasts and documentaries.

• • •

For the 2020 American Country Music Awards, Taylor did her own hair and makeup.

• • •

During quarantine, Taylor said her favourite Netflix binge shows were *Dawson's Creek* and *The Office*.

• • •

Taylor was the first solo female artist to win the VMA for Best Director, for *The Man*.

> **If something's toxic and it's only ever really been that, *just move on*.**
>
> — *Taylor Swift*

Taylor recorded her song *Peace* in one vocal take in the studio.

• • •

When her friend Gigi Hadid had a baby, Taylor gave her a handmade teddy bear made from one of her own dresses. She called it 'Ugly Bear'.

• • •

Taylor is not just musically creative. She loves painting flowers in watercolour and landscapes in oil paint.

• • •

Taylor is the first artist to have number one hits on the *Billboard Hot 100 Country Songs* chart in the 2000s, 2010s and 2020s.

Folklore was released on 7/24 and 7+2+4=13. She loves her lucky number 13!

• • •

During the pandemic, Taylor cut her own hair.

• • •

Taylor keeps a folder of favorite words and phrases which she can turn to for inspiration when she's songwriting.

• • •

All the photos taken for Taylor's *Folklore* and *Evermore* albums were shot on film. The photographer she chose, Beth Garrabrant, only uses film.

> "You can find *romance* in your life even if you aren't involved in a **romance**.

— *Taylor Swift*

Taylor said that *Folklore* represents spring and summer, while *Evermore* reflects fall and winter.

• • •

Taylor recorded and released her single *Christmas Tree Farm* within two days of writing it because she didn't want to have to wait until the following Christmas.

• • •

Taylor doesn't have Twitter on her phone because it stresses her out.

> **You don't have to forgive and forget to move on, you just become *indifferent*.**
>
> — *Taylor Swift*

Taylor didn't try her first burrito until she was 26! Now she likes to put tortilla chips in them to make them crunch.

• • •

As well as re-releasing many of her own songs in 2021 and 2022, Taylor has featured in four songs by other artists: *Renegade* and *Birch* by Big Red Machine, a remix of Haim's *Gasoline* and Ed Sheeran's *The Joker and the Queen*.

• • •

Taylor has a part in the film *Amsterdam*, which will be released in November 2022.

In 2022, entomologists named a new millipede species, *Nannaria swiftae*, after Taylor!

• • •

At New York University, cultural studies students can take a whole course on Taylor Swift called *Taylor Swift's Literary Legacy (Taylor's Version)*.

• • •

In 2022, Taylor received an honorary Doctor of Fine Arts degree from New York University.

• • •

Taylor's song *This Love (Taylor's Version)* was featured on the Amazon Prime Video series *The Summer I Turned Pretty*.

Taylor Swift Quiz
EARLY LIFE

How much do you know about Taylor's early life? Let's find out!

1. Who taught Taylor Swift how to play three chords on guitar when she was 12?

2. What is the title of the poem that Taylor Swift wrote during the fourth grade that won a national poetry contest?

3 What year was Taylor born?

4 What is Taylor's middle name?

5 Who does Taylor consider to be her biggest influence?

6 If Taylor wasn't a singer, what has she said she would do as a career?

7 What high school did Taylor attend in Nashville?

8 What was the name of Taylor's first album?

9 What is Taylor's star sign?

10 What is Taylor's brother's name?

"Everybody has that point in their life where you hit a ***crossroads*** and you've had a bunch of ***bad days*** and there's different ways you can deal with it and the way I dealt with it was I just turned completely to ***music***."

— *Taylor Swift*

11 How old was Taylor when she moved to Nashville?

12 What was the first song Taylor wrote?

13 Where was Taylor born?

14 Who inspired Taylor to become a singer?

15 Who is Taylor's BFF from high school?

16 How old was Taylor when she signed a publishing deal with Sony/ATV Music?

17 What is Taylor's shoe size?

18 What was Taylor's grade point average in high school?

THE ULTIMATE TAYLOR SWIFT FAN BOOK

19 How tall is Taylor?

20 What instruments does Taylor play?

21 What was the first thing Taylor did when turned 18?

22 How old was Taylor when she first kissed a boy?

23 What type of bug did Taylor have to knock off Christmas trees when she was younger?

24 What time of day was Taylor born?

Never believe anyone who tells you that you don't *deserve* what you **want.**"

— *Taylor Swift*

25 Taylor loves Disney movies. True or false?

26 What type of bug is Taylor scared of?

27 What hospital was Taylor born in?

28 Which town in Tennessee did Taylor move to with her family when she was 14?

29 Taylor's original demo tapes included covers of Dolly Parton. True or false?

Answers

How many did you get right?

1. A computer repairman and local musician, Ronnie Cremer.
2. 'Monster in my closet'.
3. 1989.
4. Alison.
5. Shania Twain.
6. A novel writer, interior designer, neurologist, or psychologist.
7. Henderson High School.
8. Taylor Swift.
9. Sagittarius.
10. Austin.
11. Fourteen.

12. So Happy.

13. Reading, Pennsylvania

14. Marjorie Finlay, her maternal grandmother who is a professional opera singer.

15. Abigail Anderson.

16. Fourteen.

17. 8.5 US.

18. 4.0.

19. 5'11".

20. Guitar, banjo, ukulele, and piano.

21. Registered to vote — online and in her pajamas.

22. Fifteen.

23. Praying mantis.

24. 8:36 am.

25. True.

26. Beetles.

27. Brampton Civic Hospital, room 18.

28. Hendersonville.

29. True.

THE ULTIMATE TAYLOR SWIFT FAN BOOK

Taylor Swift Quiz
MUSIC

Now it's time to test your knowledge on her music and career! Are you ready? Good luck!

1 What award did Taylor win at the 2021 MTV Europe Music Awards?

2 How many *Billboard Music Awards* has Taylor won?

3 What is the name of Taylor's Netflix documentary, which was released in 2020?

4 How many *Grammy Awards* has Taylor won?

5 What was Taylor's first single?

6 What is the name of the character Taylor played in the movie *Cats*?

7 What name did Taylor almost call her album *Lover*?

8 Which award did Taylor win at the 2022 *iHeartRadio Music Awards*?

9 What two songs has Taylor written for children with cancer?

10 Which song is Taylor's favorite to perform

11 What is the name of the song Taylor wrote for Miley Cyrus?

12 What was the first song Taylor wrote for *Folklore*?

13 What song did Taylor write for her mom as a Christmas present?

14 What song won't Taylor perform because it makes her cry?

15 What song did Taylor write when she found out her friend was battling bulimia?

THE ULTIMATE TAYLOR SWIFT FAN BOOK

"**You are not the opinion of someone who doesn't know you.**"

— *Taylor Swift*

16 In which years did *Time* magazine name Taylor as one of the world's most influential people?

17 What are Taylor's nine studio albums?

18 What are Taylor's favorite songs to sing in karaoke?

19 Which mega-celebrity described Taylor as a "*great writer*"?

20 Where did Taylor perform her first concert on her *Reputation* tour in May 2018?

21 What date did Taylor release her album *Evermore*?

What song did Taylor write as a last-minute

22 addition to *Fearless* after she broke up with Joe Jonas?

23 Taylor has won the *Album of the Year* award at the Grammy's three times. Which albums won?

24 How many units of *Folklore* were sold in its first week of release?

25 In which movie did Taylor make her feature film acting debut?

26 What fake name was used to hide Taylor's collaboration with Calvin Harris on *This is What you Came For*?

What was the first single released from her

27 *Evermore* album?

28 How many awards did Taylor win at the 2021 *American Music Awards*?

29 At which celebrity couple's house did the photoshoot for Taylor's *Folklore* album took place?

30 What was Taylor's first number 1 single on the US *Billboard* charts?

31 Who did Taylor write *We Are Never Ever Getting Back Together* about?

32 Can you name three songs Taylor wrote about Harry Styles?

33 Which were the first two albums re-recorded and re-released by Taylor?

34 What was the first re-recorded single from her back catalog, which Taylor released in February 2021?

35 How many *Country Music Awards* has Taylor won?

36 How many nominations did Taylor receive at the 2022 *Grammy Awards*?

37 How many *Teen Choice Awards* has Taylor won?

38 What was the first single Taylor released from her *Lover* album?

Answers

How many did you get right?

1. *Best US Act.*
2. 29.
3. Miss Americana.
4. Eleven.
5. Tim McGraw in 2006.
6. Bombalurina.
7. *Daylight.*
8. Best Lyrics for *All Too Well (10 Minute Version)*.
9. The unreleased '*Gracie*' and the charity single '*Ronan*'.
10. *Love Story.*
11. *You'll always find your way back home.*
12. *My tears ricochet.*
13. *The Best Day.*
14. *Never Grow Up.*
15. *Tied Together with a Smile.*
16. 2010, 2015 and 2019.

17. Taylor Swift, *Speak Now, Fearless, Red, 1989, Reputation, Lover, Folklore,* and *Evermore.*
18. Grease songs, Shania Twain and Dixie Chix.
19. Neil Young.
20. Glendale, Arizona.
21. December 11, 2020.
22. *Forever and Always.*
23. *1989, Fearless* and *Folklore.*
24. Two million.
25. Valentine's Day, in 2010.
26. Nils Sjöberg.
27. *Willow.*
28. Two.
29. Blake Lively and Ryan Reynold's.
30. *We are never ever getting back together.*
31. Jake Gyllenhaal
32. *Out of the Woods, Style* and *I knew you were trouble.*
33. *Fearless* and *Red.*
34. *Love Story (Taylor's Version).*
35. Eight.
36. One.
37. 26.
38. Me!

Taylor Swift Quiz
PRIVATE LIFE

What does Taylor get up to when she's not performing? Let's find out what you know!

1 When was Taylor first seen in public with Joe Alwyn?

2 Who do people think Taylor wrote several songs on her album *Fearless* about?

3 Which mega-company did Taylor successfully complain to about receiving music royalties from?

4   Where does Taylor's boyfriend, Joe Alwyn come from?

5   Who broke up with Taylor over the phone in about 27 seconds?

6   What was the name of the book that Taylor wrote when she was a child?

7   What blood type is Taylor?

8   Which long-haired musician did Taylor have a crush on, and wanted to marry, when she was younger?

9   How many houses does Taylor own?

10 Who did Taylor endorse in the 2020 US Elections?

11 What are Taylor's Twitter and Instagram handles?

12 What two global airlines did Taylor partner with during her *Red Tour*?

13 What are Taylor's parents' names?

14 Which singer/songwriter did Taylor's parents name her after?

15 What was the name of Taylor's ex-boyfriend who she wrote *Tim McGraw* for?

16 What song did Taylor write for a boy she was in love with but he only saw her as a friend?

"There are two ways you can go with pain: You can let it ***destroy*** you or you can use it as ***fuel*** to drive you...."

— *Taylor Swift*

17 What nickname was given to Taylor by the media while she was dating Taylor Lautner?

18 To which Tennessee charity did Taylor donate $1 million in 2020?

19 How many millions of Instagram followers does Taylor have (July 2021)?

20 What did Taylor do the day before her *Reputation* tour started?

21 Which magazine named Taylor one of the world's most influential women of 2020?

22 Which fellow singer did Taylor write *Bad Blood* about?

Answers
How many did you get right?

1. May 2016 at the Met Gala.
2. Joe Jonas
3. Apple.
4. England.
5. Joe Jonas.
6. A girl named girl.
7. Type o+.
8. Taylor Hanson.
9. Seven. One in Beverly Hills, two in Nashville, three in NYS & 1 in Rhode Island.
10. Joe Biden and Kamala Harris.
11. @Taylor_swift (Twitter) @Taylorswift (instagram)
12. Qantas and Air Asia.
13. Scott and Andrea.
14. James Taylor.
15. Brandon Borello.
16. *Teardrops On My Guitar.*
17. Taylor squared.
18. Tennessee Tornado Relief.
19. 169 million.
20. She invited 2,000 foster and adopted children to a dress rehearsal.
21. Financial Times.
22. Katy Perry.

Taylor Swift Quiz
EVERYTHING ELSE

It's time for the random question round! Are you ready? Let's go!

1 What is Taylor's lucky number?

2 In 2020, Taylor teased her newly-recorded *Love Story* song in an ad for which website?

3   What does Taylor's stationery say at the top?

4   What did Taylor say were her favorite lyrics from her *Lover* album?

5   Who is Taylor's favorite author?

6   What does Taylor always have in her fridge?

7   How does Taylor like her sushi?

8   What color are Taylor's eyes?

9   What is one of Taylor's favorite cooking shows?

10 Who is Taylor's favorite actress?

11 How did Taylor get a scar on her knee?

12 What is Taylor's favorite meal when she is in Nashville?

13 How does Taylor hold a pen when she writes?

14 What breed is Taylor's cat Benjamin Button?

15 Does Taylor have any tattoos?

16 What is Taylor's favorite drink?

17 At what event did Taylor sing the national anthem when she was 11?

18 Which song did Taylor re-release on May 6, 2022?

19 Where did Taylor first meet Britney Spears, of whom she is a massive fan?

20 What are Taylor's nicknames?

21 What is the name of Taylor's first perfume?

22 What song did Taylor sing to win a talent show when she was 11?

23 What type of farm did Taylor grow up on when she lived in Pennsylvania?

24 How many Golden Globe nominations has she had?

25 Which of her songs did Taylor say took the longest to write?

Answers

How many did you get right?

1. 13
2. Match.com.
3. "Sent with love and hugs from the desk of Taylor Swift."
4. "Our songs, our films, united we stand/Our country, guess it was a lawless land/Quiet my fears with the touch of your hand/Paper cut stains from our paper-thin plans."
5. Suzanne Collins.
6. Hummus.
7. She eats it with soy paper instead of seaweed.
8. Electric blue with a black tint on the outline.
9. Barefoot contessa.

10. Jennifer Lawrence

11. From a hot glue gun.

12. Sweet potato pancakes from Pancake Pantry.

13. She places the pen in between her index and middle finger

14. Scottish Fold.

15. No. She said she doesn't think she could ever commit to any single saying or symbol for the rest of her life.

16. Diet Coke.

17. Philadelphia 76ers NBA game

18. *This Love (Taylor's Version)*.

19. Britney Spears' Performing Arts Camp in 2003.

20. Tay, T-swizzle, Swiftie, T-swift & T-sweezy.

21. Wonderstruck.

22. Leanne Rimes' Big Deal.

23. A Christmas tree farm.

24. Three.

25. *All too well.*

Taylor Swift
THE LYRICS QUIZ

How well do you know Taylor's music? It won't be easy, but you got this. Here we go...

1. *Don't treat me like some situation that needs to be handled / I'm fine with my spite and my tears, and my beers and my candles*

2. *I once believed love would be burning red / But it's golden*

3   *He said the way my blue eyes shined / Put those Georgia stars to shame that night / I said, 'That's a lie'*

4   *He says he's so in love / He's finally got it right / I wonder if he knows he's all I think about at night*

5   *Cold was the steel of my axe to grind for the boys who broke my heart / Now I send their babies presents*

6   *I never grew up, it's getting so old*

7   *You booked the night train for a reason / So you could sit there in this hurt*

8 *Take the words for what they are: A dwindling, mercurial high / A drug that only worked the first few hundred times*

9 *That night we couldn't quite forget / When we decided to move the furniture so we could dance / Baby, like we stood a chance*

10 *And if I get burned, at least we were electrified*

11 *I can't decide if it's a choice: getting swept away*

12 *The road not taken looks real good now*

13   You held your pride like you should have held me.

14   But she wears short skirts / I wear T-shirts / She's cheer captain / And I'm on the bleachers

15   You said it was a great love, one for the ages / But if the story's over, why am I still writing pages?

16   You call me up again just to break me like a promise / So casually cruel in the name of being honest

17   They told me all of my cages were mental / So I got wasted like all my potential

18 *You did a number on me / But honestly, baby, who's counting?*

19 *I had a marvelous time ruining everything.*

20 *Sorry, I can't see facts through all of my fury.*

21 *Barefoot in the kitchen / Sacred new beginnings / That became my religion, listen.*

22 *I could build a castle out of all the bricks they threw at me.*

23 *So, I sneak out to the garden to see you / We keep quiet 'cause we're dead if they knew*

24   It turns out freedom ain't nothing but missing you / Wishing I'd realized what I had when you were mine

25   This is the golden age of something good and right and real

26   Like "Oh my, what a marvelous tune." / It was the best night, never would forget how we moved

27   I never miss a beat / I'm lightning on my feet

28   You got that James Dean daydream look in your eye / And I got that red lip classic thing that you like

29 *My name is whatever you decide / And I'm just gonna call you mine*

30 *But one of these things is not like the others / Like a rainbow with all of the colors*

31 *Cold was the steel of my axe to grind for the boys who broke my heart / Now I send their babies presents*

32 *Never be so polite, you forget your power / Never wield such power, you forget to be polite*

33 *And she's in my dreams / Into the mist, into the clouds*

Answers

How many did you get right?

1. Closure.
2. Daylight.
3. Tim McGraw.
4. Teardrops on My Guitar.
5. Invisible String.
6. The Archer.
7. Champagne Problems.
8. Illicit Affairs.
9. Out of the Woods.
10. Dress.
11. Treacherous.
12. 'Tis the Damn Season.
13. The Story of Us.

14. You Belong With Me.
15. Death By a Thousand Cuts.
16. All Too Well.
17. This is Me Trying.
18. So it Goes....
19. The Last Great American Dynasty.
20. Happiness.
21. Cornelia Street.
22. New Romantics.
23. Love Story.
24. Back to December.
25. State of Grace.
26. Starlight.
27. Shake it Off.
28. Style.
29. Don't Blame Me.
30. ME!
31. Invisible String.
32. Marjorie.
33. Carolina.

THE ULTIMATE TAYLOR SWIFT FAN BOOK

Taylor Swift QUOTES

Taylor is one of the smartest women we know, and she is always inspiring us with her quotes about life and love—both in real life and through her music.

Here are just a few of our favorite quotes from Tay Tay...

"I find something healing in writing about what used to be. And maybe that's because you can only have really seen something when you're looking back on it."

• • •

"I'm beginning to think that you don't find happiness from living your life looking ahead or back… that you find it when you look around."

• • •

"If they don't like you for being yourself, be yourself even more."

"Silence speaks so much louder than screaming tantrums. Never give anyone an excuse to say you're crazy."

• • •

"When you hear people making hateful comments, stand up to them. Point out what a waste it is to hate, and you could open their eyes."

• • •

"All you need to do to be my friend is like me."

"I can't deal with someone wanting to take a relationship backward or needing space or cheating on you."

• • •

"My ultimate goal is to end up being happy. Most of the time."

• • •

"Giving up doesn't always mean you're weak. Sometimes you're just strong enough to let go."

• • •

"People haven't always been there for me, but music always has."

"A letdown is worth a few songs. A heartbreak is worth a few albums."

• • •

"Anytime someone tells me I can't do something, it makes me want to do it more."

• • •

"Unrequited love is just as valid as any other kind. It's just as crushing and just as thrilling."

• • •

"You can have love all around without being in love."

"My life is a constant balance of understanding that I can't control everything. I can't control what people are going to think about me. I can't control what they are going to write about me. But I can control my actions and how I live my life."

• • •

"I've started to really take pride in being strong. In terms of being happy, I've never been closer."

• • •

"I've never thought of songwriting as a weapon. I've only thought about is a way to help me get through love, loss, sadness, loneliness, and growing up."

> "We don't need to share the same opinions as others, but we need to be *respectful*."

— *Taylor Swift*

"I think I am smart unless I'm really in love, and then I'm ridiculously stupid."

• • •

"Do not compare yourself to others. If you do, you are insulting yourself."

• • •

"My perfect date has nothing to do with the date, it's about who you're on the date with."

"I think the tiniest little thing can change the course of your day, which can change the course of your year, which can change who you are."

• • •

"I wish all teenagers could filter through songs rather than drugs and alcohol."

• • •

"Some days I totally appreciate everything that's happening to me, and some days I feel everyone's waiting for me to mess up."

"I think as we grow up, as you get older, you can't become bitter, we can't get jaded."

• • •

"My mom and I are really close. She's always been the friend that was always there. There were times in middle school and junior high when I didn't have a lot of friends. But mom was always my friend. Always."

• • •

"You actually will move on and you actually will be fine and then that's when he actually misses how incredible and special you are."

Taylor Swift
WORD SEARCH

```
W E S Z V M E Y N T E P
F E A R L E S S R E A S
R E T H I R T E E N H H
G H S D J E T F N X Y A
C T R E A D G O S G J K
N A S H V I L L E R R E
G R R A S T C K S A W I
U K L O D H A L Y M A T
R D W Q L Q D O R M D O
D Z G O R I F R E Y N F
H J G K E S N E S S B F
G S E G U I T A R R X Z
```

Can you find all the words below in the wordsearch puzzle on the left?

NASHVILLE	FEARLESS	GUITAR
GRAMMYS	CAROLINA	SHAKE IT OFF
FOLKLORE	MEREDITH	THIRTEEN

Taylor Swift
CROSSWORD PUZZLE

Answer the clues and fill in the puzzle—good luck!

Across

2. Number of Grammy awards.
5. Brother's name.
8. Character in Cat's.
9. City her boyfriend lives in.
10. Netflix documentary.

Down

1. State she was born in.
3. Name of 2017-2018 tour.
4. Month she was born in.
6. First 2020 album release.
7. Song she wrote for Where the Crawdads Sing.

THE ULTIMATE TAYLOR SWIFT FAN BOOK

SOLUTIONS

					M					
	F	E	A	R	L	E	S	S		S
			T	H	I	R	T	E	E	N	H
				E		F				A
C				D		O		G		K
N	A	S	H	V	I	L	L	E	R		E
		R			T		K	A		I
			O		H		L	M		T
				L		O		M		O
				I		R		Y		F
					N	E		S		F
			G	U	I	T	A	R		

COLOR-ME-IN!

Can't get enough?!

Visit us at
www.bellanovabooks.com
for more fun celebrity books.

And look out for the latest Taylor Swift book—we release an updated one is every year!

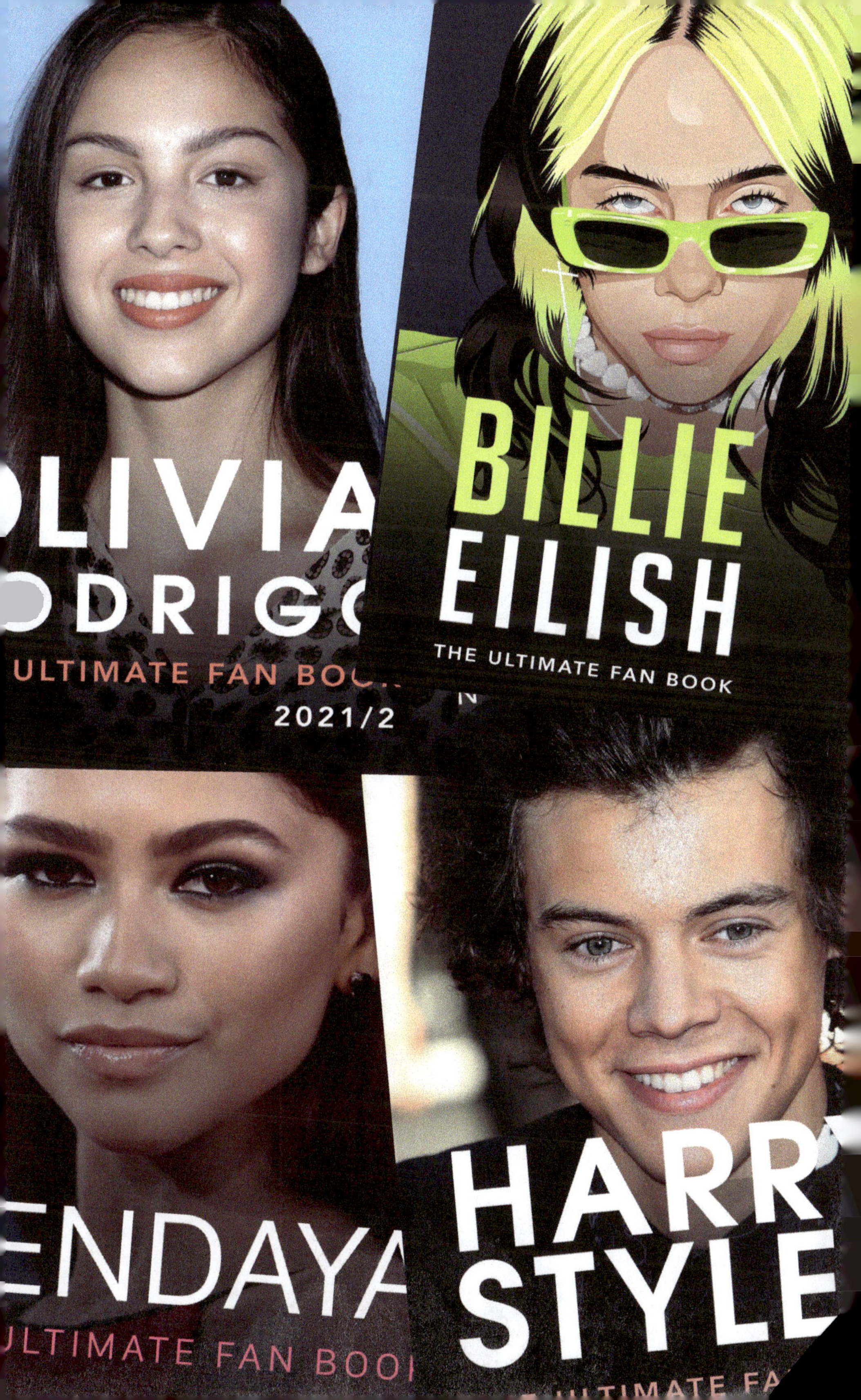

BILLIE
EILISH
THE ULTIMATE FAN BOOK

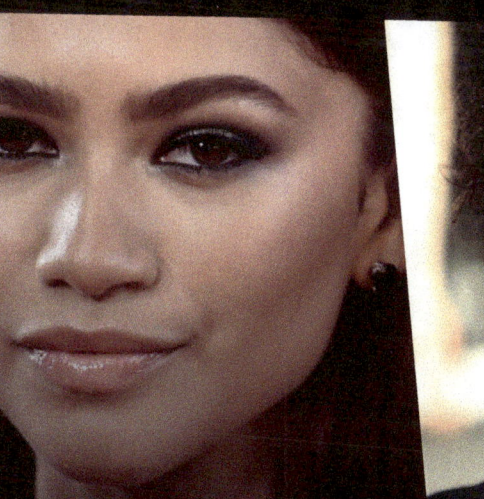

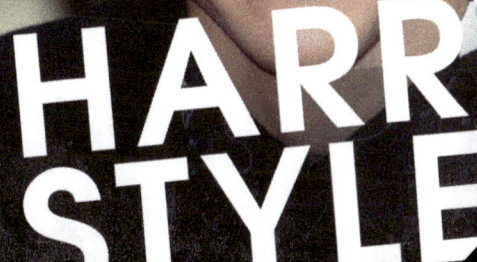

Printed in the USA
CPSIA information can be obtained
at www.ICGtesting.com
LVHW011748261123
764949LV00015B/1430